Medal of Honor Rag

A FULL LENGTH PLAY IN ONE ACT

by Tom Cole

SAMUEL FRENCH, INC.

25 WEST 45TH STREET   NEW YORK 10036
7623 SUNSET BOULEVARD   HOLLYWOOD 90046
LONDON   *TORONTO*

A PRODUCTION HISTORY

MEDAL OF HONOR RAG was telecast nationally on PBS' "American Playhouse" on the week of April 6, 1982; produced by Joyce Chopra and directed by Lloyd Richards, with the following cast:

DOCTOR .... Hector Elizondo
DALE JACKSON ("D.J.") .... Damien Leake
MILITARY GUARD .... Clarence Felder

Set design by Marjorie Kellogg; costumes by Carol Oditz.

The original stage production of MEDAL OF HONOR RAG was presented by the Theatre Company of Boston and the Fund for Theater and Film, at the New Theater in Cambridge, Massachusetts, April 14, 1975.

CAST

DOCTOR........................... David Clennon
DALE JACKSON ("D.J.") .... Gustave Johnson
MILITARY GUARD .... Paul Guilfoyle

Produced by Jan Egleson and Rikk Larsen; directed by David Wheeler and Jan Egleson.

Paul B. Berkowsky, Woodie King, Jr. and Lucille Lortel presented the first New York production at the Theatre de Lys, on March 28, 1976, with the following cast:

DOCTOR........................... David Clennon
DALE JACKSON ("D.J.") .... Howard E. Rollins, Jr.
MILITARY GUARD .... John Robert Yates

Directed by David Chambers; setting by Raymond Recht; lighting by Marshall S. Spiller; costumes by Carol Oditz; production stage manager, Dan Early.

Messrs. Berkowsky, King and Ms. Lortel presented a subsequent production at the Zellerbach Theatre, Philadelphia, in association with the Annenberg Center (University of Pennsylvania), on September 29, 1976. Jose Ferrer directed; Mr. Ferrer and Clifton Davis played the lead roles. MEDAL OF HONOR RAG has since been presented by regional theaters throughout the U.S. and in productions abroad.

The action of the play takes place in an office of the Valley Forge Army Hospital, in Pennsylvania, on April 23, 1971.

MEDAL OF HONOR RAG is performed without intermission.

NOTE

The characters in this play are fictional, but the events reported are all drawn from experiences and testimony of the period.

THE PLAYERS

DOCTOR — A white man in his early Forties, informal, hard-working (even overworked — the youngish doctor with simultaneous commitments to hospital, private patients, writing, family, research, teaching, public health, public issues, committees, special projects). White shirt and bow tie, soft jacket, somewhat weary. He is of European background, but came to this country as a child. Possessor of a dry wit, which he is not averse to using, for therapeutic purposes.

DALE JACKSON — A black man two weeks before his 24th birthday, erect and even stiff in bearing, intelligent, handsome, restrained. An effect of power and great potential being held in for hidden reasons. Like the doctor, given to his own slants of humor as a way of dealing with people and, apparently, of holding them off.

HOSPITAL GUARD — A sergeant in uniform and on duty. White. An MP, on transitional assignment.

THE SCENE

An office, but not the doctor's own office. No signs of personal adaptation — looks more like an institutional space used by many different people, which is what it is. Rather small. A desk, a folding metal chair for the patient, a more comfortable chair for the doctor. Wastebasket. Ash tray.

STAGE DIRECTIONS

With the lights still low, a squalid sound from a kazoo is heard, which flows into a rendition of the "Fixin-to-Die-Rag," by Country Joe and the Fish.

6

Medal of Honor Rag

A few verses: to bring back the mood of Vietnam
While the music plays, door opens Stage Rear and the
    DOCTOR enters. Light pours in from the corridor,
    but the DOCTOR can't find the light switch in the
    room. He feels about in half-light, then steps out-
    side again, to find the switch there. Fluorescent
    overhead light comes on, and the DOCTOR putters
    about, hurriedly, in the office. He re-arranges the
    patient's chair. Takes several folders and a notepad
    out of his briefcase.
He studies one of the dossiers *and then, after a beat,*
    looks at his wristwatch. Takes out a cigarette, filter-
    holder, and match; puts cigarette into filter and
    filter in his mouth and lights the match. Holds the
    match and lets it burn without lighting the cigarette,
    while he looks into the folder again. Puts match
    down, picks up pencil to make hurried notes in the
    dossier. *Takes a small cassette recorder out of his*
    briefcase, rummages for a cassette, checks its title,
    and puts it into recorder. Lights another match and
    this time lights the cigarette. Puts briefcase on floor
    beside the desk. Looks at watch, starts to make
    another not, takes a drag on cigarette as—
Knock on door, and DALE JACKSON enters, escorted
    by HOSPITAL GUARD. JACKSON wears
    "hospital blue denims" and slippers or soft shoes.
GUARD places paper forms, in triplicate, on
    DOCTOR's desk, points brusquely to place for
    signature. Holds out a ball-point pen to DOCTOR.

DOCTOR signs, glancing at DALE JACKSON. GUARD tears off one sheet for DOCTOR, retains others, and holds out his hand to reclaim his pen. DOCTOR hands back pen, abstractedly, and GUARD (in full Sergeant's regalia) salutes him snappily. The DOCTOR looks at the GUARD as if he were crazy. The man still stands there, at attention. DALE JACKSON watches this. Finally, the DOCTOR gets up halfway from his chair — a funny, inappropriate gesture, and waves at the man.

Doc. You can leave us alone.

Guard. (*snappy salute*) Yes, sir! I'll report back for Sergeant Jackson on the hour, sir! (*About face, marches off. The DOCTOR and DALE JACKSON look at each other.*)

Doc. Sergeant Jackson? (*DALE JACKSON nods.*) Well, they seem to be keeping a pretty close eye on you.

D.J. Where's the other doctor?

Doc. (*settling back in his chair*) Sit down, please.

D.J. They keep changing doctors.

Doc. Would you rather see the other doctor?

D.J. No, man . . . it's just that I have to keep telling the same story over and over again.

Doc. Sometimes that's the only way to set things straight.

D.J. You're not in the Army, huh?

Doc. (*twinkle*) How can you tell?

D.J. Your salute is not of the snappiest.

Doc. I came down from New York today. To see you.

D.J. I must be a really bad case.

Doc. You're a complicated case.

D.J. Like they say, a special case. I am a special case. Did you know that?

Doc. They keep a pretty close eye on you now.

D.J. I went AWOL twice. From this hospital.

Doc. Oh?

D.J. But they'll never do anything to me.

Doc. I understand.

D.J. You understand, huh?

Doc. I understand your situation.

D.J. Yeah, well, mind telling me what it is?

Doc. You don't need me to tell you that.

D.J. So what *do* I need you for?

Doc. I don't know—maybe *I* need *you.*

D.J. That's a new one. That's one they haven't tried yet.

Doc. Oh?

D.J. Every doctor has his own tricks.

Doc. Oh?

D.J. That's one of yours.

Doc. Oh? What's that?

D.J. When it's your turn to talk, you get this look on your face—kind of like an old owl who's been constipated for about five hundred years, you know, and you say (*imitation of DOC's face*), "oh?" (*The DOCTOR laughs at this, a little, but he is watching D.J. very closely. Sudden anger.*) Man, this is a *farce!* (*D.J. turns away—as if to "go AWOL" or to charge to the door . . . but he gets immediate control of himself. He is depressed.*)

Doc. (*calmly*) What should we do about it?

D.J. Who's this "we?"

Doc. Who else is there?

D.J. We just going to keep asking each other questions?

Doc. I don't know—What do you think?

D.J. What do *you* think, man? *Do* you think?

Doc. I listen.

D.J. No, man, I mean, what do you think? You got that folder there. My life is in there. I'm getting near the end of the line with this stuff. I mean, sometimes I feel like there's not much time. You know? (*As D.J. talks, he has wandered over to the desk; where he proceeds to thumb through the folders on his case. He does this with a studied casualness.*)

Doc. I'm aware of that.

D.J. You some big-time specialist? (*suddenly suspicious*)

Doc. In a manner of speaking.

D.J. What are you a specialist in?

Doc. I do a lot of work with Vietnam veterans and their problems.

D.J. Well I can *see* that, man. But what do you *specialize* in?

Doc. I specialize in grief.

D.J. (*laughs, embarrassed*) Shit. Come on.

Doc. (*as if taking a leap*) Impacted grief. That's the . . . special area I work in.

D.J. (*disgusted*) I'm going to spend another hour in jive and riddles and double talk. Only it's not even an hour, right? It's, like, impacted.

Doc. You know the word "impacted?"

D.J. How dumb do you think I am?

Doc. I don't think you're dumb at all. Matter of fact, the reverse . . . (*While speaking these words, he has opened the* dossier *to a sheet, from which he reads aloud.*) "Subject is bright. His Army G.T. rating is equilavent of 128 I.Q. In first interviews does not volunteer information—" (*Smiles to D.J., who allows himself a small smile of recognition in return; then continues reading.*) "He related he grew up in a Detroit ghetto and never knew his natural father. He sort of laughed when he said he was a "good boy" and always did what was expected of him. Was an Explorer Scout and an altar boy. . . ."

D.J. The other doctor talked a lot about depression.

Doc. What did he say about it?

D.J. He said I had it.

Doc. Oh? And?

D.J. He thought I oughta get rid of it. You know? (*The DOCTOR reacts.*) Yeah, well he was the chief doctor here. The chief doctor for all the psychoes in Valley Forge Army Hospital! See what I mean?

Doc. Valley Forge.

D.J. Yeah . . .

Doc. Why *don't* you get rid of it?

D.J. (*animated*) Sometimes that's just what I want to do! Sometimes I want to throw it in their faces! (*recollecting himself*) Now ain't that stupid? Like, whose face?

Doc. (*He is keenly on the alert, but tries not to show it in the wrong way.*) What do you want to throw in their faces?

D.J. What are we talking about?

Doc. What are you talking about? (*D.J. stares at him. He won't or can't say anything. DOC continues gently, precisely*) I was talking about depression. You said your doctor said you should try to get rid of it. I asked, simply, why *don't* you get rid of it? (*D.J. stares at him, still. He is a man for whom it is painful to lose control. He is held in, impassive.*) You meant the medal, didn't you, when you said, " throw it in their faces"?

D.J. Well. That's why you're here, right? Because of the medal?

Doc. (*gentle, persistent*) But I didn't bring it up. You did.

D.J. You asked me why I don't get rid of it.

Doc. (*repeating*) I was talking about depression.

D.J. No. You meant the medal.

Doc. *You* meant the medal. I never mentioned it . . . Are you glad you have it?

D.J. The depression?

Doc. No. The medal.

D.J. (*laughs*) Oh, man . . . Oh, my . . . Suppose I didn't have that medal . . . You wouldn't be here, right? You wouldn't know me from a hole in the wall. I mean, I would be invisible to you. Like a hundred thousand other dudes that got themselves sent over there to be shot at by a lot of little Chinamen hiding up in the trees. I mean, you're some famous doctor, right? Because, you know, I'm a special case! Well I am, I am one big tidbit. I am what you call a "hot property" in this man's Army. Yes, sir! I am an authentic hero, a showpiece. One look at me, enlistments go up 200% . . . I am a credit to my race. Did you know that? I am an honor to the city of Detroit, to say nothing of the state of Michigan, of which I am the only living Medal of Honor winner! I am a feather in the cap of the Army, a flower in the lapel of the military—I mean, I am *quoting* to you, man! That is what they say at banquets, given in *my* honor! Yes, sir! And look at me! *Look at me!!* (*pointing to himself in the clothing of a sick man, in an office of an Army hospital*)

Doc. I'm here because you're here.

D.J. What?

Doc. You ask, would I be here if you hadn't been given that medal. But if you hadn't been given that medal, you wouldn't be here, either. If my grandmother

had wheels she'd be a trolley car. You know, it's a big
"if . . ."

D.J. Yeah, but I'm saying a different "if." If a trolley
car didn't have wheels it still wouldn't be nobody's
grandmother. It would just be a trolley car that couldn't
go nowhere. Am I right?

Doc. (*after a pause*) You're right . . . (*brisk, again*)
Do you still have stomach pains?

D.J. Yup.

Doc. Nightmares?

D.J. Yup.

Doc. Same one?

D.J. Yup.

Doc. (**reads from folder**) "An anonymous soldier
standing in front of him, the barrel of his AK-47 as big
as a railroad tunnel, his finger on the trigger slowly
pressing it."

D.J. That's the one.

Doc. Who is that anonymous soldier?

D.J. You know who that is.

Doc. No, I don't.

D.J. Ain't you done your homework? (*pointing to
folder*)

Doc. My memory is shaky. . . . Please?

D.J. That's the dude who should have killed me.

Doc. "Should have?"

D.J. Would have.

Doc. What happened?

D.J. He misfired.

Doc. And?

D.J. And that's it.

Doc. That's what?

D.J. That's it, man. What do you want—a flag that
pops out of his rifle and says "Bang?"

Doc. They say you then beat him to death with the butt of your weapon . . . In combat, near — Dakto.

D.J. That's what they say.

Doc. That is what they say.

D.J. So I have heard.

Doc. What else have you heard?

D.J. That I showed "conspicuous gallantry."

Doc. You're quoting to me?

D.J. That is what they say, at banquets given in my honor.

Doc. It's part of the citation. Is it not?

D.J. (*quoting; far-away look*) Con-spicuous gallan-try, above and beyond the call of duty . . . (*with Texas accent*) "Ouah hearts and ouah hopes are turned to peace . . . as we assemble heah . . . in the East Room . . . this morning . . ."

Doc. Lyndon B. Johnson?

D.J. You got it.

Doc. What did you feel?

D.J. Nothing.

Doc. But when he hung the medal around your neck, you were crying.

D.J. See, you *done* your homework!

Doc. Are you going to poke fun at me for the whole hour?

D.J. Anything wrong with fun?

Doc. Dale —

D.J. D.J.! People call me "D.J." That's in the folder, too.

Doc. D.J.

D.J. Yes, Doctor?

Doc. Do you want to listen to me for a moment?

D.J. You said *you* was the one to listen.

Doc. I can't listen if you won't tell me anything!

D.J. I am *telling* you, man! If I knew what to tell to make me feel better, I woulda done it a long time ago. I ain't the doctor, I can't cure myself . . . (*pause*) Except one way, maybe.

Doc. (*gently, after a beat*) What are you thinking of, right now?

D.J. Nothing.

Doc. No image? Nothing in your head?

D.J. It doesn't have nothing to do with me.

Doc. But *you* thought of it.

D.J. It's about other guys, in The Nam. Stories we used to hear.

Doc. Yes?

D.J. "Standing up in a firefight . . ." (*DOC waits.*) We used to hear this . . . combat story. I wasn't in much combat, did you know that?

Doc. Except for Dakto.

D.J. Yeah. These guys, in their tenth or eleventh month — you know, we had to be there for 365 days on the button, right? Like, we got fed into one end of the computer and if we stayed lucky the computer would shit us back out again, one year later. These grunts — that's what we called the infantry . . .

Doc. I know.

D.J. I was in a tank, myself.

Doc. What happened to these grunts you heard about?

D.J. Ten months in the jungle, their feet are rotting, they seen torture, burnings, people being skinned alive — stories they're never going to tell no doctor, believe me. . . . Like, *you* never seen anything like that, right, so you can't comprehend this . . . (*The DOCTOR starts to say something in rebuttal, but then waits.*) You never seen your best friend's head blown right off his body so you can look right down in his neck-hole. You never seen somebody you loved, I'm telling you like I mean it, somebody you *loved* and you get there and it's nothing but a black lump, smells like a charcoal dinner, and that's your friend, right? — a black lump. You never seen anything like that, am I right?

Doc. (*quietly*) If you say so.

D.J. Well, *look* at you, man! Look at you, sitting there in your . . . suit!

Doc. What's wrong with my suit?

D.J. Ain't nothing wrong with your suit! . . . It's the man wearing the suit. That's what we are talking about!

Doc. You were telling me a story. (*The DOCTOR seems to show some satisfaction here — that D.J.'s feelings are beginning to pour out, even if obliquely.*)

D.J. A story?

Doc. (*looking at words he has jotted down*) About grunts . . . "standing up in a firefight."

D.J. (*as if puzzled that he was recalling this*) Oh. Yeah. So, they been through all these things, and they stayed alive so far, they kept their weapons clean, kept their heads down under cover, and then in the middle of a big firefight with 50-caliber rounds, tracers, all kinds of shit flying all over the place, they'll just stand up.

Doc. They stand up?

D.J. Yes, start firing into the trees, screaming at the enemy to come out and fight. . . . Maybe not screaming. Just standing straight up.

Doc. And? (*writing*)

D.J. Get their heads blown off.

Doc. Every time?

D.J. Oh, man — *guaranteed!* You know how long you last standing up that way?

Doc. A few seconds?

D.J. You're a bright fella.

Doc. So, why did they stand up?

D.J. (*retreating again*) Yeah, why?

Doc. Why do you think they stand up?

D.J. I don't know. You're the doctor. You tell me.

Doc. What made you think of it just now?

D.J. I don't know.

Doc. What do you feel about it?

D.J. Nothing.

Doc. Nothing . . . (*Silence, for a moment. The DOC-TOR gets up, restless, takes a step or two—looks at DALE JACKSON, whos sits, immobilized.*) D.J., I am going to tell you a few things. Right away.

D.J. (*perking up*) You're breaking the rules, Doc.

Doc. So be it—sometimes there is nothing else to do.

D.J. I mean, how do you know I won't report you to your superior?

Doc. (*smiling*) My superior?

D.J. Don't shrinks have superiors? There must be a Shrink Headquarters somewhere. Probably in New York.

Doc. Probably.

D.J. So, I'll report that *you* did all the talking and made me—a psycho—take notes on everything you said. Here, man—(*He sits down in DOC's place at desk, takes pad and pen, sets himself to write.*) I'm ready. Tell me, how do you feel now that you're going to get busted into the ranks, emptying bedpans and suchlike? . . . Oh?

Doc. (*He leans forward, to· make his words take hold.*) You see what's happening: we are playing games with each other. Because that's easy for you, and you are good at it. You could fill this hour, the week, the month that way until it really *is* too late! Do you understand that?

D.J. Do you?

Doc. How dumb do you think I am?

D.J. (*trace of a smile*) I ain't decided yet. I don't have a folder on you with your scores in it.

Doc. Yes. You're a very witty man, very quick — as long as the things we touch on don't really matter to you. But when they do, you go numb. You claim to feel nothing. Do you recognize what I'm saying?

D.J. (*dull*) I don't know.

Doc. Even your voice goes flat. Can you hear the sound of your own voice?

D.J. (*flat*) I don't know.

Doc. Do you see that?

D.J. What?

Doc. I merely *mentioned* the fact that you go numb — and you did! What do you think about that?

D.J. Nothing.

Doc. Nothing! You think nothing about the fact that you just go one-hundred-percent numb, like a stone, in response to everything that matters most in your own life? (*The DOCTOR surreptitiously glances at his watch. They are well into the hour.*)

D.J. Well, now I *am* going to tell you something, man! (*breaks out, as if he had been cornered*) I don't know why I'm in this hospital! I don't know why I'm in this room!

Doc. Then why don't you leave it? We're not getting anywhere.

D.J. (*mocking*) You mean I don't have to stay here till my hour's up?

Doc. No. I'm not your Commanding Officer. So, go.

(*D.J. does start to go. But he stops on the way to the door to return to the doctor's desk. There, he picks up the various folders and drops them into the wastebasket. He does the same thing, pointedly, with the doctor's pen. He stares at the DOCTOR for a moment, then walks to the door, opens it, and steps out into the corridor. The DOCTOR watches him, then heaves a sigh, leans on the desk to think about what has happened. But D.J. appears again at the door.)*

D.J. If I go out there, I'll be in the corridors. I hate the corridors. You ever walk the corridors of this place?

Doc. Never had that pleasure.

D.J. There's seven miles of them. Lined with basket cases. And I've walked them all, man. I've walked them all . . .

Doc. So you're going to stay here with me just to keep out of the corridors for a while?

D.J. That's right.

Doc. (*not forcing the issue*) Fine. Make yourself comfortable.

(D.J. smiles, goes to his chair, settles in, stretches, takes off his robe and/or slippers, wiggles his toes, watches his bare feet as if they were amusing animals. Begins to do a musical beat on the chair, ignoring the DOCTOR. The DOCTOR calmly goes back to the wastebasket, extracts his folders and notebook, shakes the ashes off them. He takes out his pen, taps it against the side of the basket, in counter-rhythm to D.J.'s beat, and blows the dust off. Then the DOCTOR settles comfortably at his desk, lights a cigarette, whistles a bit of the Mozart G-minor Symphony, begins to look through the folder as if to do some work on his own.)

Doc. Do you mind if I read a bit? To pass the time?

D.J. (*cool*) Help yourself.

Doc. (*After a beat; musingly*) Here's an interesting story . . . a case study I've been working on . . . trying to write it out for myself . . . about a certain man who was an unusual type for the world he came from. (*reads from or refers to folder, as if in discussion of a neutral matter*) Rather gentle, and decent in manner . . . almost always easygoing and humorous. Noted for that. As a kid in a tough neighborhood, he had been trained by his mother to survive by combining the virtues of a Christian and a sprinter: he turned the other cheek and ran faster than anyone else. . . . (*D.J. is beginning to listen with interest.*) This man was sent by his country to fight in a war. A war unlike any war he might have imagined. Brutal, without glory, without meaning, without good wishes for those who were sent to fight and without gratitude for those who returned. He was trained to kill people of another world in their own homes, in order to help them. How this would help them we do not really know. He was assigned to a tank and grew close with the others in the crew, as men always do in a war. He and his friends in that tank were relatively fortunate—for almost a year they lived through insufferable heat, insects, boredom, but were never drawn into heavy combat. Then one night he was given orders assigning him to a different tank. For what reason?

D.J. There was no reason.

Doc. There was no reason.

D.J. It was the Army.

Doc. It was the Army. The next day, his platoon of four M-48 tanks were driving along a road toward a place called Dakto, which meant nothing to him. Suddenly they were ambushed. First, by enemy rockets, which destroyed two of the tanks. Then, enemy soldiers came out of the woods to attack the two tanks still in commission. This man we were speaking of was in one of those tanks. But the tank with his old friends, the tank he would have been in—

D.J. Should have been in.

Doc. —the tank that he might have been in—that tank was on fire. It was about sixty feet away, and the crew he had spent eleven months and twenty-two days with in Vietnam was trapped inside it. . . . (*D.J. looks away, in pain.*) He hoisted himself out and ran to the other tank. Speaking of standing up in a firefight . . . Why he wasn't hit by the heavy crossfire we'll never know. He pulled out the first man he came to in the turret. The body was blackened, charred, but still alive. That was one of his friends.

D.J. He kept making a noise to me, over and over again. Just kept making the same noise, but I couldn't find where his mouth was. . . .

Doc. Then the tank's artillery shells exploded, killing everyone left inside. He saw the bodies of his other friends all burned and blasted, and then—for 30 minutes, armed first with a 45-caliber pistol and then with a submachine gun he hunted the Vietnamese on the ground, killing from ten to twenty enemy soldiers (no one knows for sure)—by himself. When he ran out of ammunition, he killed one with the stock of his submachine gun.

D.J. He kept making this same noise to me . . . over and over.

Doc. (*after a pause*) When it was all over, it took three men and three shots of morphine to quiet him down. He was raving. He tried to kill the prisoners they had rounded up. They took him away to a hospital in

Pleiku in a straitjacket. Twenty-four hours later he was released from that hospital, and within 48 hours he was home again in Detroit, with a medical discharge. . . .

D.J. My mother didn't even know I was coming . . .

Doc. Go on.

D.J. (*looking up*) You go on.

Doc. That is the story.

D.J. That's not the whole story.

Doc. What happened when you got back to this country?

D.J. What do you mean, what happened?

Doc. One day you're in the jungle. These catastrophic things happen. Death, screaming, fire. Then suddenly you're sitting in a jet airplane, going home.

D.J. They had *stewardesses* on that plane! D'you know that?

Doc. Oh?

D.J. *Stewardesses,* for shit's sake, man! They kept smiling at us.

Doc. Did you smile back?

D.J. (*straightforward*) I wanted to kill them.

Doc. White girls?

D.J. That's not the point.

Doc. Are you sure?

D.J. A white guy would have felt the same way I did. I . . . wanted to throw a hand grenade right in the middle of all those teeth.

Doc. Do you think that was a bad feeling?

D.J. Blowing up a girl's face, because she's smiling at me? Well, I'll tell you, man, it wasn't the way my mother brought me up to be. Not exactly.

Doc. Neither was the war. Was it?

D.J. Doc. Am I crazy?

Doc. Maybe a little bit. But it's temporary . . . It can be cured.

D.J. *You* can cure me? (*stares at him*)

Doc. I didn't say that.

D.J. Yeah, but you mean it, don't you?

Doc. What was it like when you touched ground, in this country?

D.J. You actually think that you can cure me!

Doc. Did they have a Victory Parade for you?

D.J. *Victory Parade?!*

Doc. Soldiers always used to get parades, when they came home. Made them feel better.

D.J. Victory parades! Man. . . . (*laughs at the insane wonder of the idea*)

Doc. You mean there wasn't a band playing when you landed in the States?

D.J. Man, let me tell you something—

Doc. You didn't march together, with your unit?

D.J. Unit? What unit?

Doc. Well, the people you flew back with.

D.J. I didn't know a soul in that plane, man! I didn't have no *unit*. Any unit I had, man, they're all burned to a crisp. How'm I supposed to march with that unit?—with a whiskbroom, pushing all these little black crumbs forward down the street, and everybody cheering, "There's Willie! See that little black crumb there? That's our Willie! No, no, that there crumb is my son, Georgie! Hi, Georgie. Glad to have you home, boy!"? Huh? . . . What are you talking about?! This wasn't World War Two, man, they sent us back one by one, when our number came up. I told you that!

Doc. People were burned to a crisp in World War Two.

D.J. Yeah, well there was a difference, because I *heard* about that war! When people came back from that war they *felt* like somebody. They were made to feel *good*, at least for a while.

Doc. That's just what I was thinking.

D.J. Then why didn't you just say it?

Doc. I'd rather that you said it.

D.J. Were you in that war?

Doc. I remember it — very well.

D.J. And you knew guys who had a parade with their unit?

Doc. I did. Banners. Ticker tape.

D.J. (*laughs at the thought*) Oh, man. How long ago was that?

Doc. Where did you land?

D.J. Seattle.

Doc. Daytime? Night?

D.J. Night. (*a pause*)

Doc. Nothing?

D.J. Nothing, man. Nothing. (*pause*)

Doc. I had one patient who got spat on, at the Seattle airport.

D.J. Spat on?

Doc. For not winning the war. He said an American Legionnaire, with a red face, apparently used to wait right at the gate . . . so he could spit on soldiers coming back, the moment they arrived.

D.J. What are you telling me this for?

Doc. Then, inside the terminal there was a group of young people screaming insults. White kids, with long hair. (*No reaction from D.J. The DOCTOR watches him carefully.*) Do you want to know why they were screaming insults?

D.J. No, Doctor, I do not.

Doc. For burning babies.

D.J. I didn't burn no babies! (*D.J. begins to pace. He is agitated. The DOCTOR watches, waits.*) The day I arrived, like, everything was disorganized. There was a smaller plane took us to the nearest landing strip, know what I mean? — and then you had to hitch a ride, or whatever, to find your own unit.

Doc. Are you talking about Seattle?

D.J. No, man. In The Nam. Like, my first day over there. My *first day,* mind you! So, I hitched a ride on this truck. About six or seven guys in it, heading toward Danang. I was a F.N.G., so I kept my mouth shut.

Doc. F.N.G.?

D.J. (*He pulls his chair up closer to the DOCTOR's desk, as if to confide in him, and he sits.*) A F.N.G. is a Fucking New Guy. See? They all pick on you over there, they hate you just because you're new. Like, nobody trusts you for the simple fact that you never been through the miseries they been having. At least, not yet . . . — Then you get friendly with your own little group, see, your own three or four friends — the guys in my tank — and they mean everything to you, they're like family — they're like everything you got in this world — I — see, that was the — thing about — that was the — . . .

(*DALE JACKSON suddenly can't go on. He buries his face in his hands and is attacked by a terrible grief — ambushed by it. He tries to pull his hands away to speak again, but it is impossible. He sobs, or weeps, into his hands. The DOCTOR hesitates, then goes around to the chair where D.J. sits, and stays there by him for a moment. He begins to lay a hand, lightly, on D.J.'s shoulder, so that D.J. will not be completely alone with his grief. But D.J. breaks away, violently. He heads away, as if to escape. The DOCTOR moves to block another impetuous exit, but D.J. had no clear intention. He is*

*frozen, sobbing. If his face is visible, it is painful to
see. The DOCTOR watches him intently, almost
like a hunter. He seems to be gauging his moment,
when D.J. will be just in control enough to hear
what the DOCTOR is saying. But still vulnerable
enough for a deep blow to be struck. Finally:)*

Doc. Is it the tank? (*D.J. cannot really answer.*) Can
you say it? (*D.J. almost begins to speak, but the catch
in his throat is still there. He will break down again, if
he speaks. He shakes his head.*) Do you want me to say
it? (*D.J. cannot answer.*) You don't know why you are
alive and they are dead. (*D.J. watches.*) You think you
should be dead, too. (*D.J. listens, silent. At times he
tries to run away from the words, but the DOCTOR
stalks him.*) Sometimes you feel that you *are* really
dead, already. You can't feel anything because it's too
painful. You dream about the rifle that should have
killed you, with the barrel right in your face. You don't
know why it didn't kill you, why just that rifle should
have misfired . . . (*D.J. hangs on these words.*) And
what about those orders that transferred you out of their
tank? Why just that night? Why you? Why did the ambush come the next day? . . . There must be something
magical about this, like the AK-47 that misfired for no
reason. Perhaps you made all these things happen, just
to save yourself. Perhaps it is all your fault, that your
friends are dead. If you hadn't been transferred from
their tank, then somehow they wouldn't have died. So
you should die, too.

D.J. (*bellowing*) I'm dead already!

Doc. (*quieter*) Yes. You *feel,* sometimes, that you are
dead already. You would like to die, to shut your eyes
quietly on all this, and you don't know who you can tell

about it. You keep it locked up like a terrible secret . . .
(*D.J. remains silent. The DOCTOR's words have the
power to cause great pain in him. After a pause.*) This is
our work, D.J. This is what we have to do.

D.J. I can't, man! I can't!

Doc. You can. I know you can.

D.J. (*stares at him; then:*) How do you know all this?
From a book?

Doc. I've been through it.

D.J. *You* were in The Nam?

Doc. No. But I had my own case of survivor guilt.

D.J. That's jive and doubletalk! Don't start that shit
with me.

Doc. It's just shorthand to describe a complicated
. . . sickness. It's the kind of thing that can make a man
feel so bad that he thinks he wants to die.

D.J. Where'd you get yours?

Doc. You think it will help you to know that?

D.J. Man, I take off my skin, and you just piss all
over me! And . . .

Doc. You want me to take my skin off, too. That's
what you want?

D.J. I want to get better! I don't want to be crazy!

Doc. Yes. That's why I'm here, to—

D.J. (*cutting him off*) You're not here!

Doc. I'm not?

D.J. There's something here. And it's wearing a
bowtie. But I don't know *what* it is . . .

Doc. Well, in this treatment, that's the way it works.
Normally it's better that you *not* know about your doctor's personal—

D.J. *Normally?!* Man, this ain't normally!

(*The DOCTOR considers this, as a serious proposition.*

Historically, The abnormal war. The desperation of this man. And he goes ahead, against his own reluctance.)

Doc. All right. All right . . . I wasn't born here. I'm from Poland. I had a Jewish grandmother, but I was brought up as a regular kid. All right? . . . Life in Poland tends to get confusing. Either the Russians or Germans are always rolling in, flattening the villages and setting fire to people. You've got the picture? Anyway, World War II came, the Nazis, the SS troops, and this time the Jewish kids were supposed to be killed—sent to Camps, gassed, starved, worked to death, beaten to death. That was the program . . . I didn't think of myself as Jewish. We didn't burn candles on Friday night, none of that. I wasn't Jewish. But my mother's mother was. So, to the Nazis I was Jewish. So, I should be dead now. I shouldn't be here. You're looking at someone who "should" be dead, like you . . . See? (*D.J. nods. He listens intensely.*) They sent me to one of those Camps. But I was saved, by an accident . . . You understand what I'm saying? Someone came along—a businessman—and he said he would buy some Jewish children, and the Nazis could use the money for armaments, or whatever. A deal. One grey morning—it was quite warm—they just lined us up, and started counting heads. When they got to the number the gentleman had payed for, they stopped. I got counted. The ones who didn't—my brother and sister and the others—they all died. But not me. For what reason? *There was no reason* . . . So, that's it. Eventually, I ended up over here, I lied about my age, got into the Army at the end of the War. I thought I wanted revenge. But now I know that I wanted to die, back over there. To get shot. But I failed. Came back, and I even marched in a Victory Parade, with my unit! So I was luckier than you, D.J. . . . But still, I didn't know why I hadn't died when everyone else did. I thought it must have been magic, and that it was my fault the others were dead — a kind of trade-off, you see, where my survival accounted for their deaths. My parents, everybody. I became quite sick. Depressed, dead-feeling . . .

D.J. How did you get better?

Doc. The same way you will.

D.J. I thought you was going to cure me.

Doc. No. Essentially, you are going to cure yourself.

D.J. Wow. (*shakes his head*)

Doc. Others, men like you, have gone through such things, and they have gotten better. That might make you feel a little better, too, for a start.

D.J. Yeah, misery loves company. Right?

Doc. Nothing magical happened, D.J. None of this was your fault. (*glances at his watch*)

D.J. How much time we got left, Doc?

Doc. Don't worry about the time. We have all the time we'll need.

D.J. You're the one is always stealing a look at your watch!

Doc. It's just a bad habit. Like picking my nose.

D.J. I ain't seen you picking your nose.

Doc. You will. You will

D.J. I guess that gives me a little something to look forward to, in my hospital stay.

Doc. (*laughs*) I guess it does.

D.J. A treat instead of a treatment. (*The DOCTOR is no longer amused. He stares at D.J., expectantly. D.J. grows uneasy.*) You want something from me.

Doc. Mm. The truck.

D.J. The truck?

Doc. The story of the first —

D.J. (*interrupting*) What truck?

Doc. There was a truck.

D.J. A truck . . . ?

Doc. First day in Vietnam. F.N.G. You hitched a ride in a truck.

D.J. Jesus.

Doc. Don't feel like talking about it?

D.J. No. I don't.

Doc. That's as good a reason as any for telling me.

D.J. (*Reacts to this notion, but then goes along with it. Sits down again, as he gets into the story.*) Well, uh . . . we were riding along, in the truck. Real hot, you know, and nobody much was around . . . and we see there's a bunch of kids, maybe three, four of them crossing the road up ahead . . . You know?

Doc. How old were they?

D.J. Well, it's hard to tell. Those people are all so *small,* you know? — I mean, all dried-up and tiny, man . . . Maybe ten years old, twelve, I don't know . . .

Doc. And?

D.J. Well, we see they're being pretty slow getting out of the road, so we got to swerve a little bit to miss them. . . . Not a lot, you know, but a little bit. This seems to make the guys in the back of the truck really mad. Like, somebody goes, "Little fuckers!" You know? . . . Then those kids, as soon as we pass, they start laughing at us, and give us the finger. Know what I mean? (*D.J. gives the DOCTOR the finger, to illustrate. The DOCTOR starts to laugh, but then puts his hand to his head, as if knowing what is to come.*) Yeah. So I'm thinking to myself, "Now where did they learn to do that? That ain't some old oriental custom. They musta learned it from our guys." . . . Suddenly the guys on the truck start screaming for the driver to back up. So he jams on the brakes, and in this big cloud of dust he's grinding this thing in reverse as if he means to run those kids down, backwards. The kids start running away, of course, but one of 'em, maybe two, I don't know, they stop, you see, and give us the finger again, from the side of the road. And they're laughing . . . So, uh, . . . everybody on the truck opens fire. I mean, I couldn't believe it, they're like half a platoon, they got M-16's, automatic rifles, they're blasting away, it sounds like a pitched battle, they're pouring all this firepower into these kids. The kids are lying on the ground, they're dead about a hundred times over, and these guys are still firing rounds into their bodies, like they've gone crazy. And the kids' bodies are giving these little jumps into the air like rag dolls, and then they flop down again . . .

Doc. (*very quiet*) What happened then?

D.J. They just sorta stopped, and me and these guys drove away. (*DOC waits.*) I'm thinking to myself, you know, what *is* going on here? I must be out of tune. *My first day in the country,* and we ain't even reached the Combat Zone! I'm thinking, like, this is the enemy? Kids who make our trucks give a little jog in the road and give us the finger? I mean, come on, man! . . . And one guy, he sees I'm sort of staring back down the road, so he gives me like this, you know—(*D.J. simulates a jab of the elbow.*) and he says, "See how we hose them li'l motherfuckers down, man?" Hose 'em down. You like that? . . . And they're all blowing smoke away from their muzzles and checking their weapons down, like they're a bunch of gunslingers, out of the Old West . . . (*D.J. shaking his head. He still has trouble believing he saw this.*)

Doc. (*measured*) Why do you think they did all that?

D.J. I don't know. They went crazy, that's why!

Doc. Went crazy . . . Were all those soldiers white?

D.J. I don't remember.

Doc. What do you think?

D.J. (*a little dangerously*) I think some of them were white.

Doc. (*Waits. D.J. does not add anything.*) And what did you do?

D.J. What do you mean, what did I do?

Doc. Well, did you report them to a superior officer?

D.J. (*explodes*) *Superior officer?!* What superior officer? Their fucking lieutenant was *right there in the fucking truck,* he was the first one to open fire! I mean what are you talking about, man? Don't you know what is going on over there?

Doc. Why get mad at me? I didn't shoot those children.

D.J. (*confused, angry*) God *damn. . . !* (*glaring at the DOCTOR*) I mean, what are you accusing me of, man?

Doc. I'm not accusing you of anything.

D.J. Well, I'm asking you! What would you have done? You think you're so much smarter and better than me? You weren't there, man! That's why you can sit here and be the judge! Right? (*No reaction from the DOCTOR, except for a tic of nervousness under the extreme tension that has been created.*) I mean, look at you sitting there in your suit, with that shit-eating grin on your face!

Doc. You're getting mad at my suit again? You think my suit has caused these problems? (*DALE JACKSON can't control his rage and frustration any longer. He blows up, grabs his chair—as the only object available—and swings it above his head as a weapon.*

The DOCTOR instinctively ducks away and shouts at him to stop; shouting—improvised.) Wait a minute! Sergeant! Stop that! (*D.J. crashes the chair against the desk, or the floor. He cannot vent his physical aggression directly against the DOCTOR. After he has torn up the room, D.J. stands, exhausted, confused, emptyhanded. While D.J. subsides:*) Are you all right? (*D.J. stares at the DOCTOR, panting. He moves away, into the silence of the room. DOC neutrally.*) How did you feel about being a killer?

D.J. *I didn't kill those kids, man!*

Doc. I didn't say you did! Did I? (*Waits. D.J. glares at him, still full of rage and suspicion. But a deep point has been made, and both men are aware of it. After a pause.*) Did you ever tell people at home about any of this? About Dakto, about the truck?

D.J. No. I didn't.

Doc. Didn't they ask? Didn't anyone ever wonder why you came home early?

D.J. Yeah, they asked.

Doc. Who asked?

D.J. My mother. Little kids, sometimes. My girl, Bea . . .

Doc. Sounds like everybody.

D.J. No, not everybody. A lot of people didn't give a shit what happened.

Doc. And you pretended you didn't give a shit, either?

D.J. What do you want me to say, man?

Doc. But what did you say when your mother or your friends asked you?

D.J. You guess. You're the specialist.

Doc. (*after a pause*) All right, I will. You said, "Nothing happened. Nothing happened over there."

D.J. Right on. Word for word.

Doc. It's in the folder.

D.J. Yeah, sure.

Doc. (*takes words from report in the folder*) It also says you "lay up in your room a lot, staring at the ceiling . . ." (*The DOCTOR waits, to see if D.J. has anything to add.*)

D.J. Read. Read, man. I'm tired.

Doc. Did you do that — did that happen to you right away?

D.J. Right away. . . ? No. Well, at first I felt pretty good. Considering . . . (*trails off*) Considering, uh . . .

Doc. Considering that you had just been heavily narcotized, tied up in a straitjacket, and shipped home in a semi-coma. After surviving a hell of death and horror, which by all odds should have left you dead yourself.

D.J. Yeah. Considering that.

Doc. You felt lucky that you had survived? At first?

D.J. I just used to like going to bars with my cousin, William . . . my friends. I was glad to see my girl, Beatrice, and my mama. I joked around with them. I tried to be good to them . . . I shot baskets with the kids, down the block. Understand?

Doc. Of course. And then what happened?

D.J. It didn't last.

Doc. And?

D.J. I started laying up in my room. Staring at the ceiling.

Doc. But what happened? What changed you?

D.J. I don't remember.

Doc. But you did go numb?

D.J. You're talking me around in circles, Doc!

Doc. I'm sorry. . . . This terrible delayed reaction, after a kind of relief — it seems so mysterious, but it's the common pattern for men who went through your kind of combat trauma . . .

D.J. (*with irony*) Well, I'm glad to hear that. But I sometimes began to suspect that my girl, Bea, might just prefer a man what can see and hear and think and feel things. And *do* things! You follow my meaning? A man what can walk and talk, stuff like that?

Doc. Did you stop have sexual relations with her?

D.J. Well, I have been trying to send you signals, man! You're none too quick on the pick-up.

Doc. Did she criticize you?

D.J. Not about that . . . She wanted me to get a job, so we could get married . . .

Doc. Well. The job situation must have been difficult in Detroit.

D.J. Especially if you lay up in your room all day, staring at the ceiling. Funny thing about the city of Detroit—not too many people come up through your bedroom offering you a job, on most days. Did you know that?

Doc. I've heard that, yes . . . Did you stop getting out of bed altogether?

D.J. No, I put my feet to the floor once in a while. Used to go on down to the V.A. and stand in line for my check.

Doc. How did they treat you down there, at the Veterans' Office?

D.J. Like shit.

Doc. Did you know why you got treated that way?

D.J. It wasn't just me personally, man.

Doc. I know. But why?

D.J. You know that a vet down the block from me flipped out last week—jumped up in the middle of his sleep and shot his woman in bed, because he thought she was the Vietcong laying there to ambush him? . . . (*The DOCTOR goes sharply on the alert at this, but waits for D.J. to continue. D.J. is profoundly uneasy about his own train of thought.*) Man, if I lose my cool again — just, freak out — what's to stop me from going up and down the streets of Detroit killing everything I see?

Doc. (*concerned, quiet*) Do you actually think you could do that?

D.J. How can you ask me that?

Doc. I'm asking.

D.J. (*charging at him*) Well what did I *do* — what did I get that medal for, man? For my good manners and gentle ways? (*They stare at each other for a tense moment. The DOCTOR starts to fit up another cigarette and filter, but throws the filter away and lights up the cigarette. Begins to pace restlessly. DALE JACKSON watches him. Then the DOCTOR abruptly turns back to D.J.*)

Doc. Tell me when you actually got the medal.

D.J. You're making me nervous!

Doc. (*keeps pacing*) As my grandmother used to say, "That should be the worst would ever happen to you."

D.J. That's the grandmother, could have been a trolley car?

Doc. *If* she had wheels.

D.J. If she had wheels. Right. (*During this colloquy — in which signs of an ease, a trust seems to be forming between them — the DOCTOR has restrained himself, but he is impatient now to pick up the thread.*)

Doc. Tell me when you actually got the medal! (*This story is relatively easy for DALE JACKSON to launch into; he settles into his old chair in the course of telling it.*)

D.J. I been home eight, nine months. Then I get this

call, they say it's some Army office. They want to know if I'm clean—if I had any arrests since I been back, you know. I tell them I'm clean and just leave me alone. Then two MP's come to the door, in uniform, scare the shit out of my mama. They just tell her they want to find out a few things about me—whether I've been a good boy—whether I've been taking any drugs. She makes me roll up my sleeves right there (*D.J. does so for the DOCTOR.*), to show—no tracks, see? When they leave, she is sure I've done something terrible, that I shouldn't be afraid to tell her, that she'll forgive me anything. And all I can do is sit there in the kitchen and laugh at her, which makes her mad, and even more sure I done something weird. . . . Well, about fifteen minutes later a Colonel calls up from the Department of Defense in Washington, tells me they're going to give me the Congressional Medal of Honor, and could I come down to Washington right away, with my family, as President Lyndon B. Johnson hisself wants to hang it around my neck, with his own hands. He'll pay for the tickets, he says.

Doc. So, another sudden ride on a jet plane.

D.J. A goddamn *Honor Guard* meets us at the airport. Beatrice is peeing in her pants, my mother's with me, my cousin, William . . . They got a dress-blue uniform waiting for me, just my size. Shoes, socks, everything. Escort, sirens. Yesterday afternoon for all they knew I was a junkie on the streets, today the President of the United States can't wait to see me. . . . (*The DOCTOR has picked up his cassette recorder while D.J. was finishing the story, and now he clicks it on. The voice of Lyndon B. Johnson plays, from the award ceremony:*)

VOICE OF L.B.J. ". . . Secretary Resor . . . General

Westmoreland . . . Distinguished guests and members of the family . . . Our hearts and our hopes are turned to peace as we assemble here in the East Room this morning. All our efforts are being bent in its pursuit. But in this company—" (*DOCTOR points the recorder at D.J.*) "we hear again, in our minds, the sounds of distant battle . . ." (*The DOCTOR turns the volume down, and the voice of L.B.J. drones quietly in the background, as he waits for D.J.'s reaction.*)

D.J. Ain't that a lot of shit?

Doc. You wept.

D.J. I don't know, I kind of cracked up. The flashbulbs were popping in my eyes, my mother's hugging me, she's saying, "Honey, what are you crying about? You've made it back." It was *weird!* (*The DOCTOR has turned the volume up again to let a few more phrases from the presidential ceremony play, giving D.J. more time for re-living the moment.*)

VOICE OF L.B.J. FROM THE CEREMONY. "This room echoes once more to those words that describe the heights of bravery in war—above and beyond the call of duty. Five heroic sons of America come to us today from the tortured fields of Vietnam. They come to remind us that so long as that conflict continues our purpose and our hopes rest on the steadfast bravery of young men in battle. These five soldiers, in their separate moments of supreme testing, summoned a degree of courage that stirs wonder and respect and an overpowering pride in all of us. Through their spectacular courage they set themselves apart in a very select company . . ." (*The DOCTOR underlines these last words—"set themselves apart in a very select company"— with a gesture. Then he flicks off the cassette recorder.*)

D.J. Weird, man.

Doc. Why was it weird?

D.J. I . . . I don't know?

Doc. You *do* know!

D.J. What are you driving at?

Doc. What did you get that medal for? (*repeating D.J.'s earlier words*) For your "good manners and gentle ways?"

D.J. (*Stares at the DOCTOR. The DOCTOR stares back.*) I got that medal because I went totally out of my fucking skull and killed everything that crossed my sight! (*pause*) . . . They say I wanted to kill all the prisoners. *Me.*

Doc. *You don't remember?*

D.J. Nothing . . . A few flashes, maybe. Those people are all so small . . .

Doc. (*He taps a finger on the cassette recorder, trying to re-capture the specific moment they have been talking about—in the White House—but he gradually gets caught up in the intense rush of his own thoughts:*) So, your mother was hugging you, in the White House, for doing what she had trained you all your life not to do—for being a killer. And everybody was celebrating you for that . . . And your dead friends from the tank, whom you had tried so hard to bury, came back again, to haunt you. You had to re-live that story, that flash of combat when a man's life is changed forever, when he literally goes crazy, psychotic, in a world of no past and no future, compacted into a few seconds, a wild pounding of the heart, blinding light, explosions, terror, and his whole earlier life slides away from him through a . . . membrane as if lost forever, and all he can do is kill—all *that* was named, broadcast, printed on a banner and waved in your own face so you can never forget . . . And you wonder why you wept, why you were confused, why you are here in this hospital? You wept for your dead friends, you wept for your dead self, for your whole life that slid away in the first fifteen seconds of that ambush on the road to Dakto. You were choking on your grief, a grief you couldn't share with anyone, and you became paralyzed by your guilt, and you still are, and you're going to be, until *you* decide to make your own journey back through that membrane into some acceptable reality . . . Some real life, of your own . . . (*Both DALE JACKSON and the DOCTOR seem momentarily stunned by the latter's outpouring.*)

D.J. I don't know how to do that, Doc.

Doc. I will tell you . . . (*glances at watch, as if recollecting himself*) D.J., do you intend to stay in this hospital for a while?

D.J. Why do you ask?

Doc. (*reads from folder for an answer*) "Maalox and bland diet prescribed. G.I. series conducted. Results negative. Subject given 30-day convalescent leave 16 October 1970. Absent Without Leave until 12 January 1971, when subject returned to Army hospital on own volition. Subsequent hearing recommended dismissal of A.W.O.L. charge and back pay reinstated . . . in cognizance of subject's outstanding record in Vietnam."

D.J. Well, yeah, they can't do anything to me.

Doc. Because of the medal?

D.J. Because of the medal . . .

Doc. (*after a beat*) I'm afraid we have only a few more minutes today. (*scanning his appointments book*) I can come down the day after tomorrow, and I'd like to talk with you again. After that, if you want, I can see you three or four times a week.

D.J. (*He automatically readies himself for the end of the hour.*) Busy man like you? (*light mockery*)

Doc. Mm-hm. But I'd like to have you transferred up to New York. I can do that, if you'll make the request . . . (*He looks questioningly at D.J. D.J. does not answer—nor does he necessarily imply a "No."*) Well?

D.J. We'll see.

Doc. We'll see what?

D.J. We'll see, when you come down again.

Doc. Can I be sure you'll be here?

D.J. You're looking for too many guarantees in life, man.

Doc. No, I'm not. I'm looking for you to make a decision about yourself. (*A knock at the door, and the HOSPITAL GUARD [Military Police Sergeant] immediately enters.*) You *can* get better, you know. . . .

GUARD. Reporting in for Sergeant Jackson, sir. (*The DOCTOR and D.J. look at each other. D.J. gets up, automatically, to go.*)

Doc. (*to GUARD*) Will you wait outside for a moment? In the corridor?

GUARD. Will do, sir. May I ask, sir, how long?

Doc. Not long. Until the interview is concluded.

GUARD. May I ask, sir, is the interview almost concluded?

Doc. The interview is almost concluded. Just giving a summation.

GUARD. Will wait in corridor, sir, until conclusion of summation of interview (*He snaps to, gives salute. The DOCTOR waves him off, with his own facsimile of a salute. The GUARD wheels into an about-face and exits to station himself outside the door, as:*)

D.J. Attaboy.

Doc. So?

D.J. So?

Doc. Do we have a deal?

D.J. Hit me with the "summation."

Doc. (*He closes up his folder.*) There is nothing to say that you don't already know. The only question is what to do about it. (*D.J. laughs.*) It was a badly damaged self that you brought back to this country, and nothing has happened here, you see, to help you —

D.J. (*cutting him off*) You're leaving a little something out, ain't you? Man, they gave me the Congressional Medal of Honor!

Doc. So they did. And what happened?

D.J. Well . . . I became a big hero!

Doc. You became a big hero . . . You appear on TV. The head of General Motors shakes your hand. You get married. You re-enlist — re-enlist! — travel around the state making recruiting speeches. You get a new car, a house with a big mortgage. Everybody gives you credit . . . for a while.

D.J. Rags to riches, man.

Doc. And then? (*D.J. makes a gesture of self-deprecation, meaning, more or less, "Here I am."*) Back to rags again.

D.J. (*challenging*) But I got the medal! Didn't that medal save me from a lot of shit?

Doc. (*beginning to pack up*) Did it ever occur to you that the medal, in some ways, might have made things worse?

D.J. *Worse?* What are you talking about, man?

Doc. Well, that's where we can begin our next session . . . If you will simply commit yourself to being here. That's all I'm asking, you know.

D.J. (*opening up the DOCTOR's folder again*) No! I want to talk about it now. I mean, it sounds like you're just getting down to the nitty-gritty, am I right?

Doc. It's all nitty-gritty, D.J. It's one layer of nitty-gritty after another, until you feel like living again. But we can't just extend this hour arbitrarily —

D.J. Why not? Just tell the cowboy out there to take a walk. You got the rank here . . .

Doc. That's not the issue. Look, for one thing I'm a little tired, too. I got up at five this morning, and —

D.J. Yeah. Well that should be the worst would ever happen to you!

Doc. All right. Let's just say for now, that it's the rules of the game, by which we *both* can —

D.J. (*pouncing on the word "game"*) So we *are* playing games! You hear?

Doc. We're playing a game for your life!

D.J. (*studies the DOCTOR*) What do you want from me, man?

Doc. I want you to get better.

D.J. No, you said you were going to tell me what I had to do.

Doc. I said that?

D.J. Yeah, you did — after a long speech about killing, when you got all excited. Probably, it slipped out, huh?

Doc. Well, that gives us something else to look into, next time.

D.J. (*sullen*) No, man. You want something from me. I been getting used to that . . . I think you're a star-fucker.

Doc. A what?

D.J. A star-fucker. Like, in the Rock world, or in the movies, these chicks who hang around close to the stars. They get their kicks, their thrills out of that.

Doc. I'm not a "chick."

D.J. But you're like one.

Doc. Meaning?

D.J. You come down here, you sniff me out. Because in your world, I'm probably a famous case. Because of my medal. Am I right?

Doc. (*gets up, and starts to escort his patient to the door*) I think we're back to where we started the hour. None of this will be easy, D.J., but I will be here the day after tomorrow, and as you say, we'll see what happens . . .

D.J. (*interrupting*) You want to take that medal away from me, don't you?

Doc. (*a little stunned*) No. Why do you say that?

D.J. Now be honest with me, man. Otherwise you're going to turn my head around backwards, for good . . . (*They look at each other for a long beat.*)

Doc. No, D.J., I don't want to take that medal, or anything else away from you. But when the time is ripe, when you are ready, you may not need it any more. That's why *you* spoke, early this hour, of wanting to get rid of it, sometimes, and of "throwing it in their faces." You see, part of you already wants to throw it away, while—

D.J. (*pulling away*) Throw it away!? (*angrily*) You're the one who's crazy. You know what I'd be without that medal? I'd be just another invisible Nigger, waiting on line and getting shit on just for being there! I *told* you about that, man! You just don't *listen!*

Doc. That's one of the very things that's driving you crazy.

D.J. What is?

Doc. That once again, in Detroit, you have been singled out from all the others.

D.J. What are you talking about?

Doc. (*pursuing him*) You know what I'm talking about! It's the same story as the tank, all over again.

Why are all the others suffering, on the streets, and only you have been spared? But you haven't been spared, and you *are* suffering . . .

D.J. So what are *you* doing? You going around telling every dude who has the Congressional Medal of Honor to just throw it away? You just dropping out of the sky into every hospital and nut house in the country, scrambling up the brains of everybody who—

Doc. (*pouncing*) You think, then, that everybody with the Medal of Honor must be in some kind of hospital?

D.J. Did I say that?

Doc. You did. You let it slip out . . . In some deep way, you agree with me.

D.J. That what?

Doc. That the medal can make a man sick—drive him into a hospital.

D.J. The whole thing makes a man sick! There's a lot of sick vets who didn't get no Medal of Honor! And they're mainlining and getting beat up in the streets and sucking on the gin bottle, and they didn't get no Bronze Star, no nothing except maybe a Purple Heart and a *"less than honorable discharge"*—bad paper, man, you can't get a job, you can't get benefits, you can't get nothing if you got bad paper. Now you tell me, what does my medal have to do with *that? (A knock on the door—on the words "bad paper, man"—and the GUARD immediately enters. Poker-faced, he listens to the end of D.J.'s tirade.)*

GUARD. Has the summation been concluded, sir?

D.J. God *damn.*

Doc. Will you please wait just a minute?

GUARD. You'll have to contact chief of section, sir, about that.

D.J. (*heated*) Didn't you hear the man? Now, fuck off!

Doc. D.J.—

Guard. Look, Sergeant. To him you're an important case, but to me you're just another nut.

D.J. (*He makes a threatening move at the GUARD.*) Just another nut. Okay . . . (*The GUARD prepares to subdue D.J. with his club, if necessary. In no time, a serious scuffle is ready to break out.*)

Doc. (*throwing himself between them*) Will both of you stop this! That's an order!

Guard. Sorry about that, sir. (*returns to parade rest; stares stonily ahead*)

D.J. I'll bet you are.

Doc. (*He looks from one to the other of these near-combatants. D.J. is still simmering, with his back to him.*) D.J. Do you watch TV here?

D.J. Some.

Doc. The news?

D.J. Not if I can help it.

Doc. You didn't see it? The other night?

D.J. What?

Doc. The medals . . . (*watching D.J. closely*) Vietnam vets. Heroes? In wheelchairs, some of them; on crutches? At the Capitol steps? Washington? Throwing their medals away? A kind of miracle-scene, like the old—

D.J. (*breaking in*) And that's what you want me to do! Hop right on down there and toss it up—

Doc. You saw it?

D.J. *I didn't see nothing!*

Doc. Some of those men . . . I happen to know some of those men . . .

D.J. You cured them?

Doc. They're curing themselves. And they're a lot like you. (*D.J. watches, non-commital.*) . . .But they refuse to stay isolated. They meet, in therapy groups, which they started. Up in New York. "Rap sessions" . . . a new kind of unit, you might say . . . Everybody tells his story. You see? They're people who have been through the same fires you have, who were *there,* whom you can trust . . .

D.J. (*after a pause*) Doc, those dudes on TV are all white.

Doc. You *have* been watching them.

D.J. Yup, and I'm going to tell you something. You got your reasons for wanting to see no more war, right? — and no more warriors. I dig that, for your sake. But a lot of folks don't want the black veteran to throw down *his* weapons so soon. Know what I mean? Like, we are supposed to be preparing ourselves for another war, right back here. Vietnam was just our basic training, see? I'm telling this to both of you, y'see, so you won't be too surprised when it comes. (*The GUARD looks to the DOCTOR for instructions.*)

Doc. (*to D.J.*) Why are you saying this right now?

D.J. I want you to have something to think about, for the next session. Give us a good starting point. . . .

Doc. Still poking fun at me?

D.J. (*He waits a moment, then smiles and gives the DOCTOR a pat on the arm.*) Don't you worry, Doc. I'll be seeing you. You just sit down now, and write your notes. In the folder.

(*D.J. walks to the door, where the GUARD momentarily blocks him, in order to give a last, official salute to the DOCTOR. The DOCTOR gives a half-despairing wave as D.J. watches. D.J. turns to the*

*door, stops, and gives the GUARD an imperious
cue to open the knob and make way for him. The
GUARD does so, grudgingly. It is a minor, private
triumph for D.J. The two exit. The DOCTOR
reflects for a moment, at his desk. Then, showing
his weariness, he packs up his belongings, gives the
room a last look, and prepares to leave. Light on
stage is reduced until he is alone in the light with
darkness around him. The feeling must be of a
change in time. The DOCTOR steps forward out of
the confines of the room, to the edge of the apron,
and addresses the audience.)*

Doc. When I drove down again from New York, two
days later, Dale Jackson did not appear for his hour of
therapy. He was in fact AWOL, back in Detroit. He in-
tended to do something about his money troubles. His
wife was in a hospital for minor surgery, and he had
been unable to pay the deposit. There were numerous
protectors he might have gone to in the city for
help—people who would not have allowed a Medal of
Honor winner to sink into scandalous debt. But he went
to none of them, this time. His wife was disturbed about
the bill. This was on the evening of April 30. He prom-
ised her that he would come back to the hospital that
night with a check, and also with her hair curlers and
bathrobe. As he was leaving, he said, "Ain't you going
to give me a kiss good-bye?" And he put his thumb in
his mouth like a little boy, which made her laugh. He
asked some friends to drive him to a place where he
claimed he could get some money, and asked them to
park—in a white section of town. He walked down the
block, entered a grocery store and told the manager he
was holding it up. He took out a pistol, but never fired a

shot while the manager emptied his own gun, at point-blank range, into D.J.'s body. Death came, a few hours later, in Detroit General Hospital, of five gunshot wounds. His body went on a last unexpected jet airplane ride to Arlington National Cemetery, where he was given a hero's burial with an eight-man Army Honor Guard. I wrote to his mother about him, about what a remarkable human being even I could see he was, in only sixty minutes with him. She wrote back: "Sometimes I wonder if Dale tired of this life and needed someone else to pull the trigger." In her living room she keeps a large color photograph of him, in uniform, with the Congressional Medal of Honor around his neck. (*Lights slow fade down to darkness, as the DOCTOR walks off. Blackout; and then lights up as the DOCTOR, DALE JACKSON, and the GUARD converge, stand side-by-side, and bow to the audience.*)

NOTE

The continuous text of Lyndon B. Johnson's ceremonial address, quoted on pp. 37 and 38 of this script, is as follows:

". . . Secretary Resor . . . General Westmoreland . . . Distinguished Members of the Congress. Distinguished guests and members of the family . . . Our hearts and our hopes are turned to peace as we assemble here in the East Room this morning. All our efforts are being bent in its pursuit. But in this company, we hear again, in our minds, the sounds of distant battle . . . This room echoes once more to those words that describe the heights of bravery in war, above and beyond the call of duty. Five heroic sons of America come to us today from the tortured fields of Vietnam. They come to remind us that so long as that conflict continues our purpose and our hopes rest on the steadfast bravery of young men in battle. These five soldiers, in their separate moments of supreme testing, summoned a degree of courage that stirs wonder and respect and an overwhelming pride in all of us. Through their spectacular courage, they set themselves apart in a very select company . . ."

This text is an excerpt from remarks made by President Johnson at a Congressional Medal of Honor award ceremony at the White House on November 19, 1968.

The address was recorded, and the tapes of the President's voice are maintained at the Lyndon B. Johnson Library in Austin, Texas.

COSTUME LIST

D.J.
blue P.J.'s
plaid robe
hospital bracelet — props
wedding ring — props
vinyl slippers
DOCTOR
3 piece suit
black wing-tip shoes
creme shirt
burgundy bow tie
black socks
GUARD
MP arm band
khaki pants and shirt
MP helmet
black belt
white belt
pistol and holder
pistol (nylon)
braid
belt loop and billy club
lapel studs (guns and U.S.)
black socks

PROPERTY PLOT

Onstage:
    1 desk — s.r.
    1 desk chair
    1 side chair — u.s. of desk facing s.r.
    2 folding chairs — s.l.
    1 standing ash tray — between folding chairs
    1 standing ash tray — u.c. behind entrance door
    1 trash can — d.s. of desk, with liner
    1 coat rack — u.r.
    1 ash tray — on desk
    pencils and matches in c. desk drawer

Offstage:
    1 clipboard with forms and pen
    1 attache case with:
        medical folder
        tape recorder and tape — preset to top
        1 medical book
        1 yellow pad
        1 pack of cigarettes
        1 book matches
        1 diary

Top of Show Check:
    rewind LBJ tape
    check batteries in tape recorder
    new liner in trash can

Personal:
    DOCTOR
        glasses
        ball point pen
        lighter

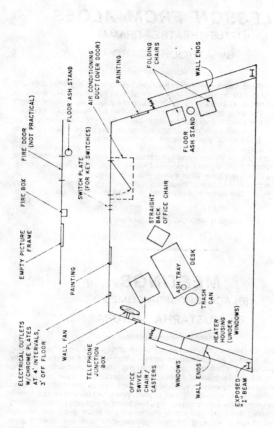

MEDAL OF HONOR RAG — GROUND PLAN

1/4"=1'(APPROX.)

APRON

Other Publications for Your Interest

A LESSON FROM ALOES
(LITTLE THEATRE—DRAMA)
By ATHOL FUGARD

2 men, 1 woman—Interior

N.Y. Drama Critics Circle Award, Best Play of the Year. Set in a house in a white district of Port Elizabeth, South Africa, in 1963 this important new work by a truly major dramatist gives a compelling portrait of a society caught in the grip of a police state, and the effect it has on individuals. We are in the house of a liberal Afrikaner and his wife. He has been actively involved in anti-apartheid activity; she is recovering from a recent nervous breakdown brought about by a police raid on their home. They are waiting for a Black family to come to dinner (in South Africa, this is an absolutely forbidden act of insurrection). The Black family never arrives; but the head of the family does. He has just been released from prison and plans to flee South Africa—after first confronting the Afrikaner with the charge that he has betrayed him. "Exile, madness, utter loneliness—these are the only alternatives Mr. Fugard's characters have. What makes 'Aloes' so moving is the playwright's insistence on the heroism and integrity of these harsh choices."—N.Y. Times. "Immensely moving."—N.Y. Post. "One of the few dramatists in the world whose work really matters."—Newsweek. (#14146)

(Royalty, $60–$40, where available.)

MEETINGS
(BLACK GROUPS—COMEDY)
By MUSTAPHA MATURA

1 man, 2 women—Interiors

Greatly-acclaimed in its recent Off-Broadway production at New York's excellent Phoenix Theatre, *Meetings* is set in an ultra-modern kitchen which would be the dream of any American family—but it is in fast-developing Trinidad and is well-stocked with everything but food, much to the consternation of the husband, a successful engineer. His wife, an equally successful marketing executive, spends too much time at "meetings" (so does he)—and neither has time to actually *use* their kitchen. While the husband pines for some good down-home cooking, the wife is off pushing a new brand of cigarette ("Trini" is being used as a test-market). Soon, the local people are coughing up blood, and many die—apparently from the effects of smoking the new cigarette. Eventually, the husband goes "back to nature" and the wife succumbs to her own product. "An amazing piece of theatre . . . a highly literal parable about the poisoning of the tropical isle by modern commercialism."—Women's Wear Daily. "A bright, sharp comedy that turns into a sombre fable before our eyes."—The New Yorker. (#15659)

(Royalty, $50–$35.)

Other Publications for Your Interest

SEA MARKS
(LITTLE THEATRE—DRAMA)

By GARDNER McKAY

1 woman, 1 man—Unit set

Winner of L.A. Drama Critics Circle Award "Best Play." This is the "funny, touching, bittersweet tale" (Sharbutt, A.P.) of a fisherman living on a remote island to the west of Ireland who has fallen in love with, in retrospect, a woman he's glimpsed only once. Unschooled in letter-writing, he tries his utmost to court by mail and, after a year-and-a-half, succeeds in arranging a rendezvous at which, to his surprise, she persuades him to live with her in Liverpool. Their love affair ends only when he is forced to return to the life he better understands. "A masterpiece." (The Tribune, Worcester, Mass.) "Utterly winning," (John Simon, New York Magazine.) "There's abundant humor, surprisingly honest humor, that grows between two impossible partners. The reaching out and the fearful withdrawal of two people who love each other but whose lives simply cannot be fused: a stubborn, decent, attractive and touching collision of temperments, honest in portraiture and direct in speech. High marks for SEA MARKS!" (Walter Kerr, New York Times.) "Fresh as a May morning. A lovely, tender and happily humorous love story." (Elliot Norton, Boston Herald American.) "It could easily last forever in actors' classrooms and audition studios." (Oliver, The New Yorker.)

(Slightly Restricted. Royalty, $50–$35)

THE WOOLGATHERER
(LITTLE THEATRE—DRAMA)

By WILLIAM MASTROSIMONE

1 man, 1 woman—Interior

In a dreary Philadelphia apartment lives Rose, a shy and slightly creepy five-and-dime salesgirl. Into her life saunters Cliff, a hard-working, hard-drinking truck driver—who has picked up Rose and been invited back to her room. Rose is an innocent whose whole life centers around reveries and daydreams. He is rough and witty—but it's soon apparent—just as starved for love as she is. This little gem of a play was a recent success at New York's famed Circle Repertory starring Peter Weller and Patricia Wettig. Actors take note: *The Woolgatherer* has several excellent monologues. ". . . energy, compassion and theatrical sense are there."—N.Y. Times. ". . . another emotionally wrenching experience no theatre enthusiast should miss."—Rex Reed. "Mastrosimone writes consistently witty and sometimes lyrical dialogue."—New York Magazine. "(Mastrosimone) has a knack for composing wildly humorous lines at the same time that he is able to penetrate people's hearts and dreams."—Hollywood Reporter.

(Slightly Restricted. Royalty, $50–$35, where available.)

Other Publications for Your Interest

THE DRESSER
(LITTLE THEATRE—DRAMA)
By RONALD HARWOOD

10 men, 3 women—Complete interior

Sir, the last of the great, but dying, breed of English actor/managers, is in a very bad way tonight. As his dresser tries valiantly to prepare him to go on stage as King Lear, Sir is having great difficulty remembering who and where he is, let alone Lear's lines. With a Herculean effort on the part of Norman, the dresser, Sir finally does make it on stage, and through the performance—no thanks to the bombs of the *Luftwaffe*, which are falling all around the theatre (the play takes place back stage on an English provincial theatre during an air raid during World War II). It is to be Sir's last performance, though: for backstage in his dressing room after the performance, the worn out old trouper dies—leaving his company—and, in particular, his loyal dresser—alone with their loneliness. "A stirring evening . . . burns with a love of the theater that conquers all . . . perfectly observed, devilishly entertaining backstage lore."—N.Y. Times. "Sheer wonderful theatricality . . . I think you'll love it as much as I did."— N.Y. Daily News. "Enthralling, funny and touching. Lovingly delineated dramatic portraits . . . Almost any actor would jump at them."—N.Y. Post. "A wonderfully affectionate and intelligent play about the theatre."—The Guardian, London.

(For Future Release. Royalty, $60–$40, when available.)

EQUUS
(LITTLE THEATRE—MORALITY)
By PETER SHAFFER

5 men, 4 women, 6 actors to play horses—Basic setting

Martin Dysart, a psychiatrist, is confronted with Alan Strang, a boy who has blinded six horses. To the owner of the horses the horror is simple: he was unlucky enough to employ 'a loony'. To the boy's parents it is a hideous mystery: Alan had always adored horses, and although Dora Strang may have been a slightly overindulgent mother and Frank Strang a slightly tetchy father, they both loved their son. To Dysart it is a psychological puzzle to be untangled and pain to be alleviated . . . or rather, given his profession, that is what it ought to be. As it turns out, it is something far more complex and disturbing: a confrontation with himself as well as with Alan, in which he comes to an inescapable view of man's need to worship and the distortions forced on that need by "civilized" society. Since this is a story of discovery, the reader's excitement would be diminished by a detailed account of its development. "The closest I have seen a contemporary play come to reanimating the spirit of mystery that makes the stage a place of breathless discovery rather than a classroom for rational demonstration. Mr. Shaffer may have been trying for just such iconography—a portrait of the drives that lead men to crucify themselves—there. Here I think he's found it."—Walter Kerr, N.Y. Times.

(Royalty, $50–$35.)